© 2021 Sassi Editore Srl
Viale Roma 122/b
36015 Schio (VI) - Italy

Text © Emanuela Durand
Illustrations and design © Leonora Camusso
Translation: SallyAnn DelVino

ATLAS OF BIODIVERSITY

ECOSYSTEMS TO PROTECT

Text
Emanuela Durand

Illustrations
Leonora Camusso

Introduction

To live well is to **be well**. There are many factors that influence the quality of life of a species: a caring family, good health, a comfortable and safe place to sleep or shelter from the elements, a pleasant environment to walk around in and spend our days, play and have fun with friends, and enough food to eat, both nutritious and tasty. What else do we need? If these conditions are met, we can say that we are in a good place in life, that **we are home**. This is why when we think of home, we think not only of the house in which we live, the room in which we sleep, but also of everything that makes us feel safe and content, that we are **in the 'right place'**. When you take a long trip, no matter how fantastic it is, after a while you feel homesick, want to return to your everyday life, to see your friends again, bicycle on your streets and sleep in your own bed. For all living beings, a 'house' is not just a landscape that acts as a backdrop to the passage of time. It is above all the **environment in which a species thrives**, interacting with all the others that live there, and finds the best conditions to make that place 'home'. If all functions well, there are no fights between neighbours or overly intrusive species: the pieces of the puzzle fit together perfectly, and everyone feels at home.

And the more species—the greater the diversity of different kinds of living beings—**the better for all of us**. There are species that adapt to living in very different and distant places, others that can survive only in particular, rare and specific places. In this book we will get to know some **wonderful habitats**, with a wealth of flora and fauna that make them truly unique. On this journey you will be accompanied by **a very special guide**, one used to moving about the world and, for this reason, well informed on many different corners of the earth.

May I present the tardigrade!

Hello to you all! I am excited to accompany you on this **wondrous exploration** of many hidden corners of our planet! I am the **tardigrade**, also commonly known as the 'water bear' or 'moss piglet'. Perhaps these names make me seem quite mysterious: I am a **very small animal**, and because of my size very few can claim to have actually seen me. To observe me, in fact, you would have to look through a microscope. But rest assured that I am here and not about to run off anywhere in a hurry: my name, in fact, means **'one who walks slowly'**. I and the many species that make up my category live **everywhere**.

We have homes across the planet, in every corner of the earth. We can consider ourselves **aquatic animals**, because we can comfortably splash around even in very little water; we live in salt and fresh water as well as on land. We can **endure** the lack of water for ten years, **extreme temperatures**, **solar radiation**, **high** and **low pressure** and the **lack of oxygen**... In fact, when we find ourselves in a difficult situation, **our body halts itself into a stasis** and only reactivates when conditions turn better. Not to sound presumptuous, but we're unbeatable!

This is why I am your guide, because I am truly **an animal of the world**.

TABLE OF CONTENTS

AMERICA

 Air temperature — **24°C**

Water temperature — **23.5°C**

Annual rainfall — **406 mm**

First stop: the ecosystem of the Galapagos Islands!

Travel by sea

I would have loved to be on the **Beagle**, the exploratory ship that reached the **Galapagos Islands** in 1835. On board was **Charles Darwin**, a naturalist. Darwin observed living beings around the world and detected that **organisms change their appearance and habits** through evolution in accordance with the environmental conditions in which they live: only those organisms that have the **traits best suited** to a particular environment survive. This change can begin by chance, from a completely **random** trait.

Miconia

Black mangrove

The luck of chance

By chance, if a small bird is born bright purple, it can be easily seen in the heart of the forest. Therefore, its species may not have a long life, because it will be easy prey. Everything suggests, therefore, that **this chance mutation will not be repeated** in future generations, because it is not **favourable** to survival. If, however, the **change** is **advantageous**—for example, it is born with a hard beak able to pierce coconuts and feed on their milk— this 'random' trait **will be repeated** in generations to come. I am not a scientist, but I understand that the discoveries of Charles Darwin have changed the way we see the world and its creatures.

Born from the sea

The Galapagos are an **archipelago**, that is, a group of many islands of volcanic origin. Some formed millions of years ago, others are still in formation. The islands are located in the **Pacific Ocean**, about 1,000 km off the coast of Ecuador, and their geographic position plays a fundamental role in **safeguarding** the great diversity and uniqueness of their inhabitants. These islands were all born from the activity of a hot spot that produces **volcanic material**, which solidifies to create islands. This spot is at rest, but the surrounding plates are still moving! (During the long history of our planet, it is these plates, like huge rafts, that moved across the oceans to form the continents.)The islands themselves, in fact, **are slowly moving**.

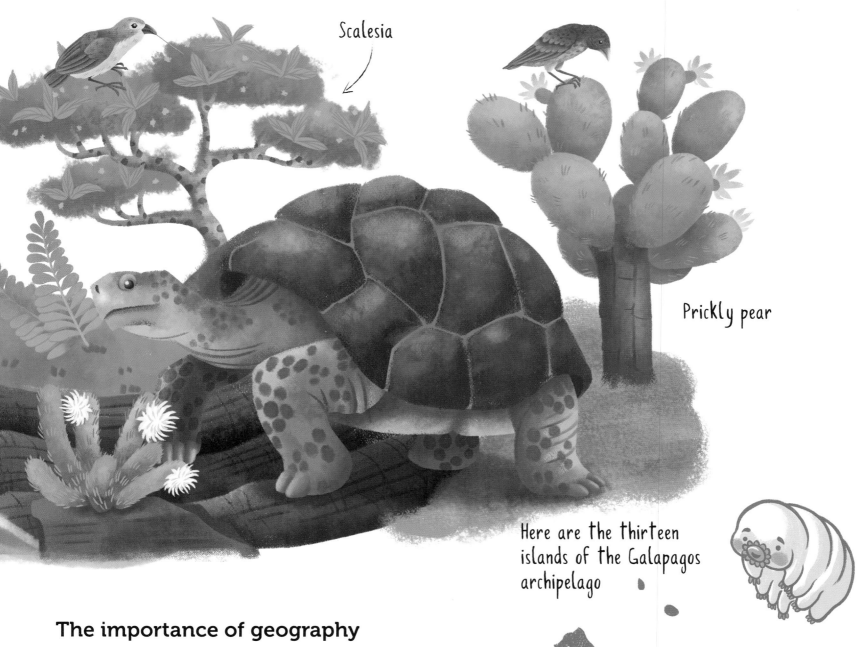

Scalesia

Prickly pear

Here are the thirteen islands of the Galapagos archipelago

Isabela

The importance of geography

The largest island, **Isabela**, straddles the equator, and its size acts as a **barrier** to a cold underwater current, called a **cold equatorial current**, pushing it to the surface. This brings with it an incredible amount of **nutrients**, feeding the numerous animal species that live in this place. If, due to drastic climate change, this current were to change direction, all these nutrients that replenish these islands would disappear, triggering a **decline** in the number of species present.

Symbolic Animal

The giant Galapagos tortoise and I share a similar slowness, but certainly not a similar size! Imagine, this animal is **over one metre** long and the males of the species can weigh up to **400 kg**. This beautiful creature is the **symbol of the archipelago**, but along with other species it is **vulnerable**, too often **threatened by humans**, who introduce domestic species that compete with it for food or that prey on its eggs.

Giant tortoise of the Galapagos Islands

Enchanted islands

The navigators of the past used this word 'enchanted' because **the sea** that surrounds the islands was so **difficult to navigate**. In another sense of the word, the Galapagos archipelago is truly magical, with its **variety and richness of species unique in the world!**

Comparison of beaks

LARGE GROUND FINCH (male)
The beak evolved
to break nuts

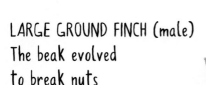

THE GROUND-DWELLING CACTUS FINCH (Female)
has a beak specialized to search for food
among cactus spines

Darwin and his finches

On the Galapagos Islands there are **13 species** of finches, all descendants of a **common ancestor** from the Americas and all which have become differentiated because of isolation and eating habits. What distinguishes them is the **shape of the beak**, which has changed according to the food consumed. Insects, seeds, nectar from cactus flowers and even seabird blood allow the finches to **divide resources fairly** and form a **large family**.

THE GALAPAGOS SINGING FINCH (male)
The smallest of the Galapagos finches
has a slender beak it uses
to look for insects among
leaves and moss

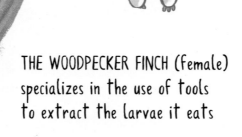

THE WOODPECKER FINCH (Female)
specializes in the use of tools
to extract the larvae it eats

A 'portentous' lichen

In the arid zone of the archipelago there is a **particular type of lichen**, used in the past to obtain a **dye**. Recent studies have shown that this species can be used in medicine as an **anticancer drug**. However, science is aware of the delicate balance of these environments, and for this reason, even if it is not endangered, this lichen is **collected sparingly**.

Daring and thorny

Another plant species exclusive to the islands is the **lava cactus**, which grows in a very short time all over the **lava zones**, standing out against the black background. It has **different colours**, ranging from golden yellow to black, because the stems darken with age. Its **thorns** are a useful survival tool that **keep it from 'sweating' water** under the scorching sun. The flowers close in the evening and then reopen at the first light of dawn.

'Repellent' reptile

At the first encounter, 'repellent' was the adjective used to describe the **marine iguana of the archipelago**, the only instance in the world of an iguana adapted to live in the marine environment. **Dark in colour** in order to better absorb the heat of the sun, it feeds on the **algae** located a short distance from shore, which it reaches by **swimming for a few minutes** in a way that prevents its body from getting too cold.

The marine iguana of the Galapagos is the only fully marine lizard

Parasitic fly in finch nests

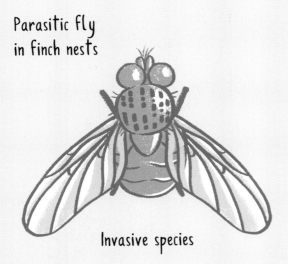

Invasive species

Questions of coexistence

The Galapagos archipelago has been designated a **UNESCO World heritage site** since 1978 and remain one of the most protected natural areas in the world. This is because **in the past humans have threatened its delicate balance**, hunting indigenous species and introducing invasive species. The idea of living in these places is attractive to many people and the number of inhabitants, as well as of tourists, has grown greatly in recent years. However, we must be careful so that **human presence is limited** in this environment, so unique in the world and governed by such fragile balances, to ensure that all its natural wealth is preserved for a very long time.

AMERICA

Who lives in this arid place?

 Air temperature **18.5°C**

 Water temperature **21.6°C**

 Annual rainfall **1-35 mm**

Rain dance

Let's just say this place is not really suitable for me... indeed it is not ideal for anyone! Outside certain areas of Antarctica, **the Atacama desert is the driest place in the world**. Imagine, in certain spots there has been no rain for decades. In short, it is a decidedly **inhospitable** place for almost all living species. After all, when imposing mountains such as the Andes act as a **barrier to rainfall from the Amazon**, the good weather in this area lasts for a long, long time. However, hills close to the coasts allow for **mist** to create less-dry zones, where life is able to develop. These misty oases are called **'lomas'**.

Rock purslane

Martian landscape

In the Atacama is a **valley** where time has carved very particular shapes. There really seems to be a different reality here: no plant life but **only sculptures modelled over the centuries**. This territory has been compared to the **land on planet Mars**, and for this reason is used by scientists to evaluate the presence of life forms or as a set for science fiction films. Well, **finding me here is not easy**: I prefer places a little less dry.

Flowering wind

Every five years in the desert a warm and embracing wind blows, **El Niño**, or **'the child'**, which reaches the Chilean coast and brings the long-awaited abundant **rains**. This phenomenon lasts a **few days**, and that is more than enough for the desert to become covered with **thousands of colourful flowers**. It is a sight unique in nature! This beauty has been **protected since 1997**, in ways in which many visitors can observe it but without causing damage.

Leucocoryne cornata

Rhodophiala phycelloides

Here you will find the 6-metre Atacama Cosmology telescope!

From day to night

As in any self-respecting desert, **the temperatures vary a lot between day and night**. When the sun goes down, the thermometer does the same, and it is not uncommon for it to drop below zero at altitude. And at night, this **area, free from light pollution**, offers a very special view of the stars in the sky. I never thought such an inhospitable place could offer such an amazing spectacle!

Attentive ears

In the driest areas of the desert, life is difficult, and in order to survive, a **good temperament** is needed! It is not uncommon to see the **chilla**, a South American grey fox with large ears, roaming the dunes. You know that foxes are generally **clever**, right? However, if it is easy to be clever in an area rich and abundant in food, it is a bit more difficult in a desert where **meals are scarce!**

Darwin's mouse

Definitely an interesting food for the chilla is a **small Chilean rodent** that lives in the same area. In such an inhospitable place, this little mouse is able to adapt by choosing **slightly rainier seasons** for periods of activity and reproduction. See, I'm not the only one who likes the rain!

Resources in the subsoil

The desert's name derives from a **mineral** in the area, **atacamite**, which, contrary to what I do, **develops only in the absence of water**. In fact, atacamite dissolves when in contact with water. The area is full of **mines to extract** this material, from which copper is obtained and used in various industries. The landscape has often been modified to make room for mining exploration, and, over the years, the **land's appearance has changed**. I really hope it won't completely change!

With a few drops of rain the desert is tinted in a thousand colours!

Colours and scents

I think you figured it out: desert plants and animals live only in certain places. So, **when the desert blooms**, as by magic, we discover **unique and rare flowers!** Some survive thanks to their **bulb**, which **acts as a food reserve** during the dry phases; when conditions improve and the long-dreamed-for rain arrives, they flower the desert in colours and scents.

A most bountiful fog!

Other plants live solely **thanks to the fog or mist**, absorbing from it the **nutrients necessary** for survival and adapting to live in an environment where there is no water. The little water present inside them, in fact, is **preserved as much as possible**, avoiding any sort of 'sweating' under the day's sun.

Tillandsia landbeckii

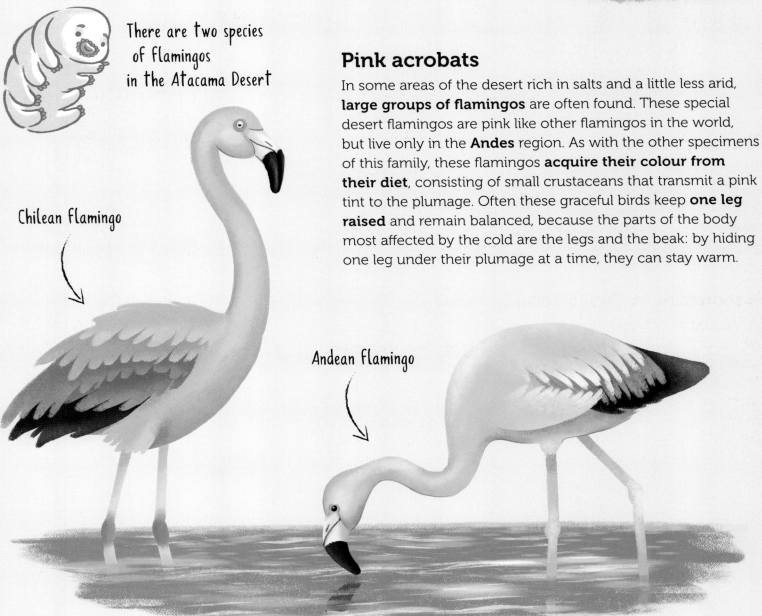

There are two species of Flamingos in the Atacama Desert

Chilean Flamingo

Andean Flamingo

Pink acrobats

In some areas of the desert rich in salts and a little less arid, **large groups of flamingos** are often found. These special desert flamingos are pink like other flamingos in the world, but live only in the **Andes** region. As with the other specimens of this family, these flamingos **acquire their colour from their diet**, consisting of small crustaceans that transmit a pink tint to the plumage. Often these graceful birds keep **one leg raised** and remain balanced, because the parts of the body most affected by the cold are the legs and the beak: by hiding one leg under their plumage at a time, they can stay warm.

Survival

Humans have always lived here, and I would dare say that there are peoples almost more resilient than I! But, just like me, they are strictly **dependent on water**, which is why they reside around the small oases of this driest desert in the world. They are the **Lickan Antai**, who have learned to survive here as farmers and ranchers, managing to bend water to their will. They are the **guardians** of these difficult lands, which in recent times have been transformed by the **exploitation of mines** and **massive tourism** from all over the world. This is the home of all the brave heroes and heroines who survive here against the dangers of the present, and it is important that this home not be damaged.

AMERICA

African river

'The Amazon is an African river? What does this mean?' you may think, 'Everyone knows the Amazon River is in South America!' No, I did not catch sunstroke. The fact is that in our time the river is located in Latin America, but in very ancient times **its source was** in what is today the country of Chad, **in Africa!** Back then, not surprisingly, India, Africa, South America, Australia and Antarctica were still united in a great super-continent called **Gondwana**. The river flowed west, into the **Pacific Ocean**. Curious, isn't it? According to some scientists it was the **longest river** the world has ever known! And then what happened? Well, everything went **geologically topsy turvy**: Gondwana broke apart. South America moved away from Africa separating the river from its source, and the Andes formed, creating a barrier. Here **the great river transformed**, changed direction and decreased in length (a length which is still considerable). With the Nile, the Amazon competes for the record of **the longest river in the world!**

Along the banks of the longest river in the world!

 Air temperature   **26°C**

 Water temperature   **28°C**

Annual rainfal   **2,300 mm**

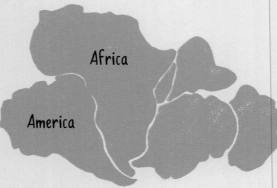

Africa

America

Victoria amazonica

16

The Brown River

The colour of the 'Mar dulce', as it is also called because of its great extent, is not beautifully clear and blue, but **brown**. In fact, at first sight it looks dirty, but in reality this colour comes from the **sediments that detach from the Andean mountains**, where the river originates, and flow in the river to the end of its course.

Flooding is beautiful

When the rains are intense, **the river swells out of its banks** and floods the forests that grow all around it. While this might sound like a cataclysm, it is actually a **blessing**. Thanks to the river water, the soil becomes **fertile** and **rich in nutrients**, allowing all species to thrive.

Cocoa plant

Brazilwood

Sound of the waves

At certain times a year, when the moon is new and full and the **ocean tide** is high, **a powerful tidal wave several metres high** travels up the river. This causes a fearsome, often **crashing sound** that frightens the inhabitants of the area, except for the few daredevil surfers who try to ride it! This river tidal wave is called by the local people Pororoca, which translated means 'great crashing sound'.

Giant otter

Great and large

In the Amazon waters the **giant otter** swims gracefully. It uses its **long tail**, which can measure up to 70 cm, also as a **weapon of defence** against attackers. Evidently, however, its tail has proved little protection against humans who for a long time **hunted** it for its dark, waterproof fur, **drastically reducing its population**. The giant otter is now a **protected species** and can often been seen swimming with others of its kind.

A high-voltage creature

In the river's waters lives a very **special fish** it would be best not to anger. The **electric eel** possesses a powerful weapon to both defend and attack: an **electric discharge** capable of stunning and killing prey much larger than itself! It lives in **waters rich in vegetation**, where it can hide and ambush its prey.

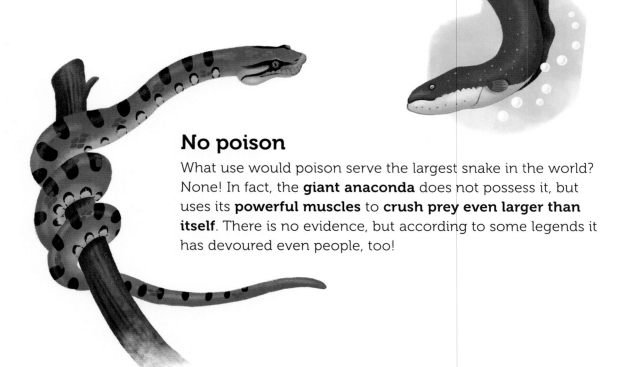

The anaconda is the largest snake in the world

No poison

What use would poison serve the largest snake in the world? None! In fact, the **giant anaconda** does not possess it, but uses its **powerful muscles** to **crush prey even larger than itself**. There is no evidence, but according to some legends it has devoured even people, too!

Tasty tree

Who among you doesn't like chocolate? Delicious, no? Well, in this area **the cocoa tree grows spontaneously** and its **fruit**, yellow and as big as a rugby ball, has the particularity of growing directly **attached to the branches and trunks**. Before being transformed into a tasty treat, its seeds undergo several processes.

Did you know that cocoa is made from a fruit?

Victoria amazonica

Like a queen

In the calmer areas of the river lives a regal plant: the **largest water lily in the world**. I bet its floating leaves could support your weight! Its white **flower** (which turns pink) is the **size of a football**. A splendour for the eye of the observer...from afar! To defend itself from the bites of water inhabitants, this plant, in fact, has a type of **thorns**.

Like leaves

I must admit, in nature there are animals skilled in the art of disguise, and the **matamata turtle** is one of them. Its colours, scaly shell and colouration allows it to **blend perfectly with its environment**. Algae even grow on its back, enabling it to blend in with the aquatic surroundings. This ability at disguise makes it a **skilled hunter**.

Matamata turtle

From paradise to purgatory

The fauna and flora that live in this corner of the world are **rare and special**, but their uniqueness is often ignored. All too frequently these treasures are **threatened by the indiscriminate cutting of forests and water pollution** by modern gold prospectors, who pour tons of mercury into the river, a liquid metal that has devastating effects on living beings. If we want these places to revive, we must do more and not let them become barren and lifeless.

EUROPE

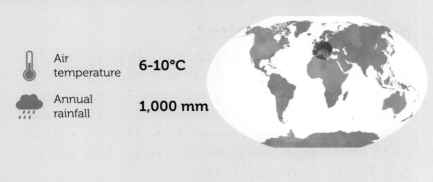

🌡️ Air temperature **6-10°C**

🌧️ Annual rainfall **1,000 mm**

Mont Blanc is the highest mountain in the Alps at an altitude of 4,808 m!

Higher and higher

We are among the mountains, specifically the most important mountain range of the European continent: **the Alps**. Mont Blanc and the other peaks are the result of a **play of interlocking between two different plates**, the **European** and the **African**. Long ago, these two plates slowly collided, causing first faint ripples and then gradually **taller and taller mountains** (which **continue to grow** even today). For you, one millimetre a year may be imperceptible, but from my point of view it is a considerable unit of measurement!

Precious and fragile reserve

The Alpine region is rich in **streams** and **small and large lakes**, which makes it an important **water reserve** for all of Europe. Furthermore, the **glaciers** present at high altitudes are a precious and important 'treasure' for all living beings. These glaciers are being closely monitored, because unfortunately **their current state of existence is not good**. These ice masses, in fact, are melting at a rapid rate because of increasing temperatures. If elsewhere the temperature has risen by an average of one degree in the last fifty years, in the Alps it has risen by **two degrees**, revealing a landscape that had previously remained hidden. I can adapt to changes in climate, but not everyone can!

Mountains to protect

On these mountains there are **many animal and plant species** that make the Alps considered one of the few **truly pristine** areas of nature in **Europe**. Already at the beginning of the 1900s it was understood that this wealth had to be **preserved and protected**, and the first **national parks** were born, the Swiss National Park in 1914 and the Gran Paradiso Park (Italy) in 1922.

Marine sediment

Europe

Africa

At the bottom of the sea!

If you visit certain areas of the Alps, you can truthfully say that you are walking **at the bottom of the ocean**. But how is this possible, given that you are in the mountains? If you look closely, you can see **fossil remains of marine organisms from past eras**. In fact, during the collision of plates, what had been in the ocean, such as fish and other organisms, emerged and **fossilized together with the rock**, which is nothing other than the ancient ocean floor.

A solitary 'big cat'

There are animals that are difficult to observe in their environment, and the **lynx** in the Alps is one of them. It roams silently and stealthily through the woods with its **large furry paws** that allow it to **move with dexterity even in the snow** without sinking...a bit like wearing snowshoes! Like other predators, the lynx has suffered **severe threat from humans**, which meant that at the beginning of the 1900s not even a single specimen remained in the entire Alpine arc. In the 1970s **specific rehabilitation programs sought to re-introduce** this species in Switzerland, Austria and Slovenia, and the lynx returned to these mountains.

European lynx

Alpine salamander

Dark is better

To live in the mountains some species have had to adapt to the sun which is very strong at high altitudes. Species of **salamander** and a **subspecies of** viper appear **completely black** because, assuming this colour, they need **less time to heat their body** and at the same time **protect themselves from the sun's rays**.

The 'petals' of the edelweiss are actually modified leaves and the real flowers are in the centre

They are covered with hairs to protect themselves from intense sunlight

A gift from the mountains

Many flowers grow in the **alpine meadows** and in springtime offer unique views to those who have the chance to observe them. But there is one flower that wins over all hearts for its resilience and longevity: the **edelweiss**. This 'alpine star' is considered the **'flower of remembrance'** and has often been collected as a token of love, brought down from the mountains to one's beloved. Its importance in the eyes of humans, however, has a price: its **steady disappearance**. To protect this treasure, the edelweiss became the **first protected flower in the world**.

Bearded vulture

Golden eagle

Rulers of the sky

Among the **birds that use warm air currents** to climb valleys and observe landscapes from above are the **golden eagle** and the **bearded vulture**. The first is a **bird of prey whose excellent eyesight** allows it to identify its prey from above (often much larger than itself), grab it with its **powerful talons** and let it fall to the ground to then feed on it. The bearded vulture, on the other hand, 'exploits' the work done by another (by predators or by time) by **eating** carrion. Both birds have a **remarkable wingspan**, although the bearded vulture boasts first place in this ranking.

Hidden treasures

Inside **encasements of rock**, **precious minerals** are often found that dazzle with their beauty. These were formed during the **birth of the Alps** as a result of chemical and physical changes within the rocks of the two plates. One such is **hyaline quartz**, also called **'eternal ice'** because, at first glance, it looks like a piece of ice...but which never melts! Observing inside the cracks and crevices of rocks, you can find a **mysterious world** that is largely yet to be discovered.

Beautiful crystal formations can be found in the alpine crevices

Humans and the mountain

These territories, often hostile to you humans, have been inhabited for a very long time. Just think, in the 1990s an exceptional discovery was made in the glaciers of Austria: a man, later nicknamed **Ötzi**, was **found perfectly preserved inside a glacier**. Humans have adapted over time to live with these mountains, although nowadays we often do not respect them as we need to. The **exploitation of the territory** and the development of **mass tourism**, in fact, deeply affect the life of the Alps.

EUROPE

 Air temperature **5°C**

 Water temperature **7°C**

 Annual rainfall **1,000 mm**

The temperature of the water emerging from a geyser is about 80-120°C

Elements in comparison

It seems a contradiction, but on the second-largest island in Europe, Iceland, ice and fire coexist. Here are found the **largest glacier on the continent** and about **thirty active volcanoes**. Those who live here are used to feeling the earth shake, spit and smoke: in short, this is **a place for the truly hardy**. If you want to observe the forces of nature in all their might, this land of contrasts is for you!

Common Eider

Young land

Iceland is a **younger territory**, formed much later than other areas of the world. Just think, within the island there is a **rift that divides two parts of the 'global puzzle'**: the European and the American plates. In this area, these plates are **moving away from each other**, which means the island continues to grow and fracture at the rate of two centimetres per year! Below the surface of the island there is a **hot spot** that draws directly from the depths of the soil and creates new substances. In the past, some believed that this point was **a direct access to the centre of the earth!**

Volcanic in nature

Because of its powerful internal disruptions, the island has often experienced **serious natural disasters**, such as volcanic eruptions and earthquakes. It is not uncommon for one of these Icelandic occurrences to **complicate life for the rest of the continent**, covering the sky with dust for days on end. But when the earth's crust is very thin, harmless spectacular manifestations can also occur, such as **geysers**, scalding hot springs that propel powerful jets of water from the surface.

Northern lights

Virtuous territory

Iceland boasts the European record as the **most environmentally-friendly**: good air quality (apart from occasional fumes), excellent use of water and geothermal resources, good forest management, careful planning of fishing and agriculture and, despite the various difficulties, a healthy diversity of living beings.

The Snow Queen

One of the few animals native to this island is the **Arctic fox**. In the winter season its **fur** is **almost completely white** which allows it to blend perfectly with the surrounding snow, while in the spring and summer seasons its coat changes appearance to a **grey-brown**, perfectly in tone with the surrounding landscape. Different from the red fox, the arctic fox has a **shorter snout** and **smaller ears**, allowing it to better adapt to the cold winter weather and avoid heat loss.

Winter fur

Summer fur

Icelandic horses are small with a long coat

At a trot

It is not uncommon to see **horses running free** on the Icelandic prairies. These belong to **a race introduced to the island** by the Vikings before the year 1000. Adaptation to the environment did the rest: **these horses have experienced a climate of warm and cold periods**, food shortages and volcanic eruptions, but all this has made them particularly **resilient!** They are beloved and jealously **protected by Icelanders**, who do not allow entry to the island of any other types of horse.

Unwanted guests

There are animals that, once brought to the island, **did very well for themselves** in taking up much more space than expected. Such is the case of the **reindeer**, brought to Iceland for breeding, or the **American mink**, introduced for its fur. **Without natural predators**, these continue to multiply and spread. When moving living beings around the world, we need to be **aware of the consequences!**

Mink

Fern growing near geysers thanks to geothermal heat

Toward Warmth

Temperatures are very hot about the geysers. Life forms develop here that prefer these extreme conditions. I'd be able to live here without any problem, and I'd find myself in the company of **organisms of my size or even smaller**, such as **certain bacteria** that need to scorch themselves a little in order to function. There is also a **particular type of fern** that grows only on the island and near these sources of heat produced by the earth.

The puffin flies at around 80 km/h and can flap its wings very fast

Dressed up for a carnival

There is a **bird** on the island that **inspires immeasurable fondness**, so much so that it has often been recast into a cartoon character: the **puffin**. This bird has legs suitable for digging, although it prefers to use burrows left free by other animals to lay its eggs underground. The puffin is a **skilled fisher** and its large beak can hold numerous fish.

Nootka lupine

Priority: plant trees

Unfortunately, **there are not very many trees** in Iceland. Indeed, we could say there are very few because of the **exploitation in the past** to obtain construction materials. At present, attempts are being made to remedy the situation by **reforestation** in some areas of the country. Most of the territory is made up of **prairies** where **lupine**—introduced from North America in the 1970s to prevent soil erosion—clearly prevails over other species. This plant has become a **problem** for some and a **resource** for others. Certainly, in summer the **purple** of its flowers does not go unnoticed.

AFRICA

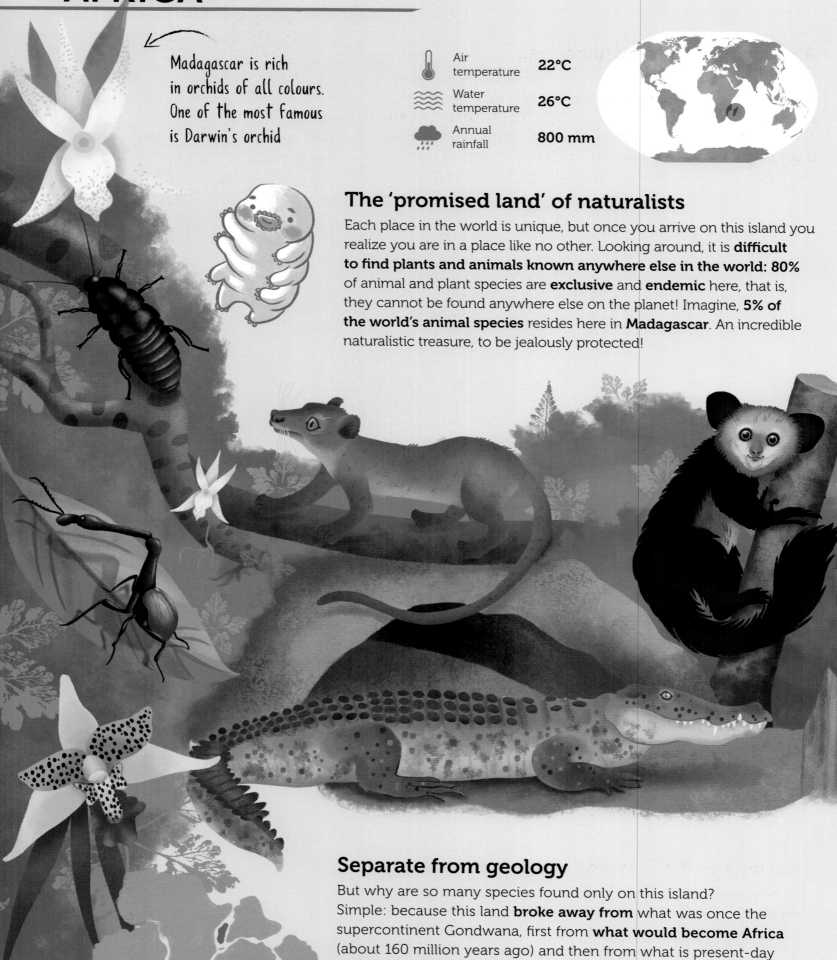

Madagascar is rich in orchids of all colours. One of the most famous is Darwin's orchid

🌡️	Air temperature	**22°C**
〰️	Water temperature	**26°C**
☁️	Annual rainfall	**800 mm**

The 'promised land' of naturalists

Each place in the world is unique, but once you arrive on this island you realize you are in a place like no other. Looking around, it is **difficult to find plants and animals known anywhere else in the world: 80%** of animal and plant species are **exclusive** and **endemic** here, that is, they cannot be found anywhere else on the planet! Imagine, **5% of the world's animal species** resides here in **Madagascar**. An incredible naturalistic treasure, to be jealously protected!

Separate from geology

But why are so many species found only on this island?
Simple: because this land **broke away from** what was once the supercontinent Gondwana, first from **what would become Africa** (about 160 million years ago) and then from what is present-day **India** (about 90 million years ago). These geological movements have led to the preservation of species on the island which had become **extinct or evolved differently elsewhere, surviving and progressing** in Madagascar without external influences.

A vast diversity of landscapes

The fourth-largest island in the world, Madagascar has a **great diversity of environments and territories**. Here we encounter **prairies** similar to the African savannas, **tropical forests**, **thorny and arid forests**, **fertile areas** exploited by humans for crops, **stunning beaches** and **inaccessible cliffs**. This diversity augments even more the great variety of species present in Madagascar!

Humans and the island

Reaching this land has never been easy because of the **strong ocean currents** along its coasts. The **first people** to land here, about two thousand years ago, were **Indonesians**. Others followed, and the amazement of those pioneers created a mixture of fear and respect for all the creatures that lived on the island. Over time, these mixed feelings have led to **some animals** being **venerated**, and others **persecuted**. Even today, **stories** and **legends** born of primordial beliefs are present in the local culture.

The satanic leaf-tailed gecko has adhesive scales to stick to trees

If the shoe fits...

One of the typical animals of Madagascar is the **lemur**, a primate found only on this island. But lemurs are not just one species: there are about **a hundred**, and each lives in a different environment. We discover, for example, the **sifakas**, which move **at ease among the thorny trees** thanks to their extremely tough pads, which protect their paws, and **'fly'** from tree to tree without a care. Crowned lemurs, on the other hand, move easily on *tsingy*, sharp formations that are the remnants of **ancient coral reefs**: 'tsingy' means 'where you cannot walk barefoot'. Evidently, with good balance some can manage it!

Some baobabs can measure up to 30 m high and 11 m in trunk circumference

Symbolic trees

On the island there are two trees that certainly do not go unnoticed: the **traveller's tree** and the **baobab**. The first is the **symbol of Madagascar**, and is so called because the base of its leaves helps travellers to **collect rainwater**. The baobab, on the other hand, is a **real giant in the plant world**. Hardy and resilient in a dry and hostile climate, it can store within itself **100,000 litres of water**, which allows it to live up to 3,000 years enduring drought. I feel so tiny in comparison!

Creatures of the dark

In the northern region of the island there is an **intricate system of underground caves** that house fearless animals, which often cause fear in humans. These **places** are considered **sacred** by the local people and are often used as **hiding** places or as **tombs** for ancient kings. Here in the semi-darkness lives the **largest centipede in the world**, which feeds on decaying vegetation carried to these depths by the waterways. In the same caves we also find the **crocodile**. It is unexpected to see it spend most of its time in the earth's darkness, especially because as a reptile it is **cold-blooded**. Why it dwells here remains a **mystery**, but it could have something to do with the level of humidity.

The crocodile that has adapted to life in the caves is a variant of the Nile crocodile

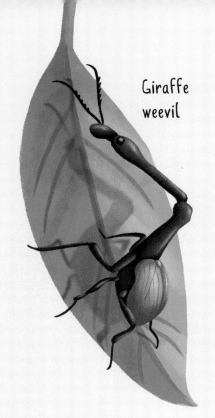
Giraffe weevil

Small world

Perhaps I have a certain fondness for smaller creatures, but on this island there are **many species of insects and spiders**. Of particular interest is the **giraffe weevil**: the males of this species **use their long neck to fight** opponents and to prove themselves worthy to female companions. Another insect is the **Madagascar hissing cockroach**, which uses its hiss as an alarm cry if disturbed. There is also a **spider** that can protect itself by creating **a shelter inside an empty shell** and anchor itself to a tree with silk it spins.

Hissing cockroach

Chameleon

Change of colour

There are creatures that can **change colour** for different necessities. There are those that, like the **satanic leaf-tailed gecko**, do it to blend in among the tree trunks, where they spend most of the day **upside down**, remaining motionless and incognito! Imagine, **half of all chameleon species** live in Madagascar and their colour is linked to their **emotions**. In short, they communicate with each other through colourful spots on their skin.

The aye-aye is a very special primate; it is the only representative of its genus and a nocturnal animal

Not everyone is safe

On this island, **the relationship between humans and nature is very strong**, but not all species are protected in the same way by local tribes and by visitors to the island. There are creatures that are **persecuted**, such as the **aye-aye**, considered a bewitched beast and omen of death, now **close to extinction**. Of other animals, such as the elephant bird, the largest bird ever to exist on Earth, **no trace remains**. Another threat to the numerous species of **amphibians** on the island is the presence of a **fungus** that has already claimed other victims in other areas of the world.

AFRICA

The Serengeti is a famous reserve of lions and elephants. Other lesser-known but very interesting animals live here, too!

 Air temperature **18°C**

 Annual rainfall **900 mm**

In search of water

Water is essential for all living beings. Those who live in certain areas of the world know they have to make **sacrifices** in order to find it, or hope that the **sky**, as happens here twice a year, decides to offer this **long-awaited gift**. Some animals, such as the **gnu, migrate in large groups** to reach 'blue gold'; **lions**, on the other hand, **stay put** and wait for water and prey to return to the territory.

Hard earth

The **savanna in Tanzania** has **various landscapes**, however with a single origin. Two million years ago, in fact, this area looked very different: over time **ash from the eruptions** of many volcanoes has been consumed, transported and sculpted by the wind. This ash has hardened to create a **layer of very solid rock**, difficult for most tree roots to penetrate, so in some areas trees are totally absent.

Hungry things come in small packages

Some of the most admired animals in the world live on the **Serengeti plain**: lions, giraffes, zebras, cheetahs, elephants and many others, common figures of many popular fairy tales and cartoons. Some of the **smaller players** on the scene **in the savanna**, however, though far more inconspicuous, **cause great damage: flies** and **ticks** torment many of the larger animals at the forefront. You might think the Serengeti's most voracious herbivores are the huge elephants, right? Rather, it is the **myriad of insects** that insatiably devour undeterred the low vegetation of the plain!

Human presence in distant times

Three and a half million years ago in this area some of the **first human beings** appear to have walked on the planet. This is confirmed by a series of **footprints** impressed **in wet ash**. The ash had solidified and was covered by another layer of the same, which served as a 'blanket' conserving this testimony until its discovery by scholars in **1978**.

Umbrella thorn acacia

A giraffe's tongue is 35 cm long!

Whistling-thorn acacia

A giraffe's saliva has disinfectant properties to protect it from injuries caused by thorns

What a tree!

Here trees are very sparse. We find especially **acacias of different colours**, with their classic **'umbrella'** shape that broadens to better capture the sun's rays. Plants and animals have moved in tandem in the course of evolution: **plants** have learned to **defend themselves** from those that wish to feast on them without restraint, while **animals** have evolved to **reach the most desirable parts of plants**. Acacias, in fact, have **thorns** and **specialized shelters** for **ants** that attack plant-eating visitors. In turn, **giraffes** have developed a **very long neck** to eat the leaves up high on the tree, changing the shape of the tree: the giraffe is a good gardener!

Klipspringer

Caracal

Bat-eared fox

To each his own ...plant

In the Serengeti there are many **herbivores** and each has learned to eat **different vegetation, different parts** of vegetation or **parts at different stages of growth** in the same plants: to avoid too much competition. **Buffalo** and **zebra** are easy-going and satisfied with **dry grass**, while **gnu** and **antelope** prefer **leaves** and **tender shoots**, which are rich sources of energy. **Thomson's gazelle**, on the other hand, prefers **short grass**.

Good neighbours

To avoid competition, animals in the Serengeti created a **'reserved' area** in which to live and eat, choosing specific foods. Among the herbivores is a small antelope, the **klipspringer**, which lives in **rocky areas** and feeds often on **succulents**. Among the carnivores, far from the crowds of lions, cheetahs, leopards and hyenas, the **caracal** jumps and preys on birds, the **ocelot** feeds on mice just like a country cat, and the **bat-eared fox** eats insects, avoiding competition with other canids. Two animals with an appetite for **termites** are the **aardwolf** and the **aardvark**, but each hunts at a different time: the aardwolf during the day and the aardvark at night.

Temminck's courser nests in the newly burned areas

Necessity of fire

It seems strange that a **fire** could **help a land**, but the nearly annual fires here do. The burning of mainly dry grasses enriches the soil with **nutrients** needed for the growth of new vegetation within a relatively short time, recycling everything in a perfect mosaic. These fires **almost never pose a threat to animals**, except for the slowest creatures. On the contrary, some animals even use them as an opportunity!

Cattle Egret

Oxpecker

Valuable work

Some **birds** do a **very important job**, freeing large herbivores from **annoying parasites** on their skin. The best known is the **cattle egret**, a large and slender bird that often and willingly follows buffalo herds, feeding on the mites on the backs of the buffalo. **Little grebes** take care of the delicate skin of hippopotami, while gnu find helpers in the **wattled starlings**. **Oxpeckers** can also specialize as **nurses**, cleaning wounds, going from back to back on this mission, sometimes taking hair as a reward to build their nest.

Little Grebe
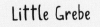

Longing for Africa

The Serengeti plain and its National Park are among the **most visited areas in Central Africa**. Its boundless nature and large animals bring **many visitors** and feed our imagination. This area was declared a **UNESCO World heritage site** in 1981, to remind humans of their responsibility to preserve these areas over time.

UNESCO is the United Nations Educational, Scientific and Cultural Organization

ASIA

Sacred sea

The environment I'm about to share with you is so big it looks like a sea, but in reality it is **fresh water**. Yes, we are talking about a lake, but it is the **largest lake on our planet!** Even more fascinating, Lake Baikal grows bigger and bigger, because **its shores** are slowly **moving away** from each other. The area is still changing and who knows if in the very distant future it will transform itself again to really become a sea. We are in **Siberia**, in northern Asia (or Russia), in a **place of extreme climate**. However, this enormous mass of water **makes the climate a little less extreme**: winter is not as cold and summer is not as hot in areas nearer the lake.

Follow me to the shores of Lake Baikal!

	Air temperature	**0.9°C**
	Water temperature	**10°C**
	Annual rainfall	**42.7 mm**

Blueberries

Rhododendron

Freshwater reserve

This lake is **a true treasure** for the whole world: if we exclude glaciers and polar ice caps, it alone constitutes **23% of the planet's freshwater reserves!** In short, for me it is a real paradise where **water is never lacking**. The lake is fed by many **rivers**, over 300, while all the waters leave the lake through a single outlet, **Angara**.

The maximum depth of this basin is **over 1,600** m with a surface area of **31,500 km²**, larger than the whole of Belgium. Even given its great depth and size, for about six months a year the lake is **completely frozen over**, but life below the surface continues.

Like a mirror

The waters of Baikal are **crystal clear**, so transparent that in some spots it is possible to see to the bottom! The depths are **rich in oxygen**, and **internal motions** move the waters in such a way to support organisms living even at **low depths**.

Siberian spruce   Siberian fir

The waters of Lake Baikal are rich in oxygen

Humans and the environment

In this habitat we find **unique species** not found elsewhere, which have **adapted** and **coexist** with the largest lake in the world. Humans have lived here for centuries. In fact, **ancestral depictions** of hunters and gatherers dating back to the **Neolithic Era** have been found at the southern part of the lake. This means that the wilderness of these places has been settled since ancient times: **living here**, even with its many difficulties, **is possible**, while respecting and protecting this **magical environment**.

New life

If one day you want **to explore our planet** and go in search
of new living species, Lake Baikal is just the place for you.
Imagine, **new living organisms** are discovered here **every
year**. Of course, they are mostly **microscopic**, **difficult to find**
and live mainly in **water**, but with the right studies and a keen
eye, anything is possible! **Happy searching!**

Rear fins

Freshwater seal

It looks the same as all the others, but it is not: the **nerpa**, the
only seal that lives in fresh water, exists only in this place.
Observing it closely, you will see some **differences** compared
to its 'saltwater' cousins: it is a little **smaller** and its **rear fins
are different**. Here, on the waters of the Baikal, the nerpa is
the undisputed leader of the lake, all fish belong to it without
competition from any other species. How the nerpa got here
is a mystery: it was probably isolated from other seals by
the force of the planet's moving land masses. Here, this seal
adapted to fresh water, but must live with what is often the
adversary of many species: humans.

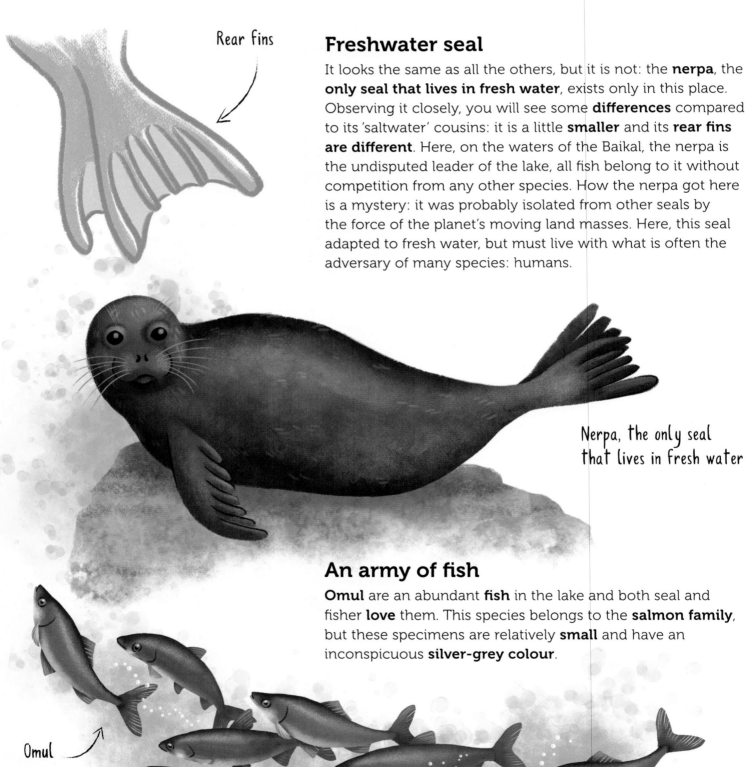

Nerpa, the only seal
that lives in fresh water

An army of fish

Omul are an abundant **fish** in the lake and both seal and
fisher **love** them. This species belongs to the **salmon family**,
but these specimens are relatively **small** and have an
inconspicuous **silver-grey colour**.

Omul

Absorbing is beautiful

Strange organisms live on the lakebed and are true keepers of the water's health and beauty. They are **sponges**, and at first glance they look like **underwater forests**. In reality they are **beings formed by other beings**, a collection of microorganisms that live together to form a perfectly functioning structure helping to **keep the lake healthy**. In fact, these sponges, by their nature, **filter the water** of Baikal, purifying it and keeping it clean.

Lake Baikal sponge

The sponges appear green because of the algae that cover them with which they live in symbiosis

Marsh thistle

Great forest

Near the lake the **vegetation** is **typical of the forests** of this region of the planet. We are in the **taiga** (boreal forest), where **tall conifers** tower above tasty **blueberries** and colourful **rhododendrons** in the undergrowth. If we move towards the **banks**, instead we find **marsh thistle** covering large areas, often spreading perhaps a little too much.

Protected

Around the lake live several **animals typical of the Arctic taiga**, but one in particular stands out among all: the **sable**, a small mammal that, in the past, because of its fur, was highly prized by many, including Russian nobles. For this reason, since 1915 it has been designated an **endangered species**, and the **strict restrictions** that prevented its hunting have meant that this animal is still **present today in the Siberian forests** and beyond.

Sable

Thanks to conservation efforts, sables are no longer endangered

Sick lake

Human beings are curious. You like to travel and discover, but often your curiosity leads to **missteps**, especially when visiting fragile places like Lake Baikal. One of the problems of maintaining the integrity of this environment is **tourists**, too often **not very respectful** when visiting places like this. Problems include **pollution** which adds to the **fever** the entire planet suffers from, making the **lake sick** and endangering all the species that inhabit it.

ASIA

The Borneo forests are some of the richest in biodiversity in the world!

Air temperature	22.9°C	
Water temperature	29°C	
Annual rainfall	220.5 mm	

Grand island

Let's go back to a region of the world that I particularly like because it is **rich in humidity**: we are on a large island in **Asia, Borneo**. This island is the **third-largest island in the world** and for its biodiversity is a gift of the whole earth. Here too, as in other areas of the world, living **species continue to be discovered**, mostly of **small size**. As you may know, we tiny creatures are many and we are often ignored because we are too small to see.

The forests are composed of trees belonging mainly to the Dipterocarpaceae family

Ancient forest

At one time the whole island was covered with an **incredible forest uncontaminated** by human presence, which today we call a **'primary forest'** or **'old-growth forest'**. Within, **plant life has remained the same** as ever, following cycles of nature unaffected by human activity. Trees will age and die, and **organisms will decompose** them making the soil ready to welcome new life. Every corner of this happy oasis welcomes **many forms of life**, which need their home to remain as they have always known it.

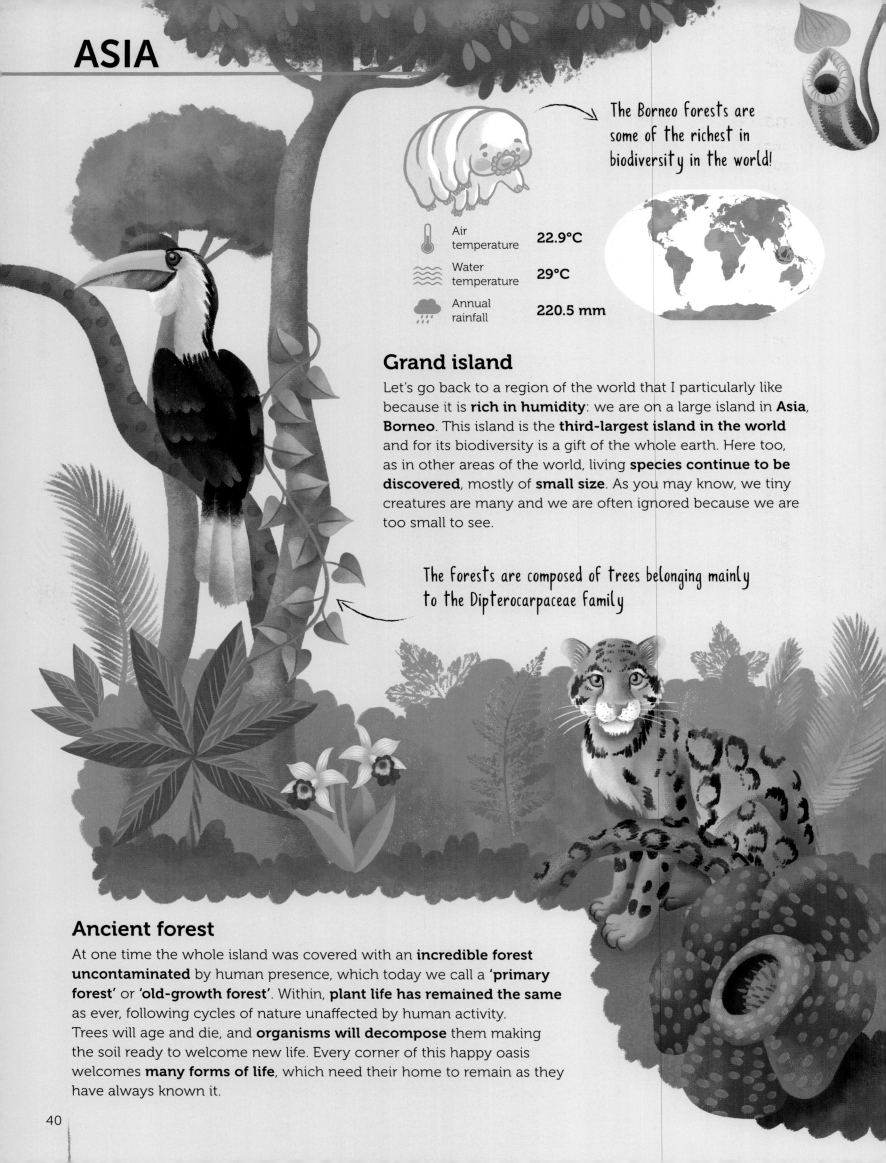

FOREST OF BORNEO

Human greed

Humans have destroyed the balance of this idyllic and perfectly functional place. The discovery of **precious resources in the subsoil**, such as coal, oil, gold and diamonds, have attracted many people. **The island has never been the same since**. The forest has changed drastically. Many old-growth trees have been cut down to make way for large areas to be exploited. The **favourable climate** has attracted the interest of large industrial groups that have removed trees to make space for other **species to be cultivated**, especially for **palm oil**, used all over the world. Within a few years, this island has suffered **serious losses** that can never be recovered. Just think, one-half of the old-growth forest has already been **lost forever!**

From the sea to the mountains

In Borneo it is possible to observe the **various layers of the forests**, because there are **many types of different environments**. On this large island you can travel from the sea to as high as 4,000 metres on **Mount Kinabalu**, the tallest mountain in Borneo. Such different environments at different altitudes host **many species**, very distant from each other which often **do not** even **come into contact**: one of the great riches of this **unique place in the world!**

41

The humans of the forests

In the forests live the **orangutans of Borneo**, a species that belongs to our large family, the **primates**. Thanks to their long arms, orangutans move nimbly among the tree branches. Their **reddish fur** is long on their shoulders, almost like a cape to shelter from the rain. Orangutans spend most of their time in trees where they build shelters with fronds. They eat **a lot of fruit** abundant in the forest. Do you understand how much trees are essential to their home and their survival? Tragically, because of the destruction of the forests, in recent years we see **fewer and fewer Bornean orangutans**.

Humans and orangutans share 97% of the same DNA!

The nose knows

The **proboscis, or long-nosed, monkey** that lives on the island is smaller than the orangutan, but just as good at moving through the trees or mangrove forests near waterways. In addition to being an **excellent climber**, it is also a **skilled swimmer**, even though moving in the waters is dangerous because of the presence of predators, such as **crocodiles**. A peculiarity that immediately catches the eye is the male's **large hanging nose**. This oddity allows the male to **instil fear** in other males and inspire **amazement** in the females.

All poison

Among the less conspicuous species we find some very curious ones, such as the **kamikaze ant** and a **red caterpillar**. The first, when it feels threatened or in serious danger, **explodes in a cloud of poison**, dying but also killing its predators. The second, a moth caterpillar, manages to build a cocoon with the **poisonous resin** of a forest tree: in this way, no predator dares to taste it.

This ant defends itself with a very special method!

Stinking flowers

In the forest there is a **special plant without roots** and **leaves**, which gets its nourishment from other plants.
This plant also sports a record: it produces **the largest flower in the world**, at 110 cm in diameter, the size of a coffee table! If you are expecting a pleasant scent from this blossom, you will be sorely disappointed: **it smells of rotting meat**. Unfortunate only to our human noses, the scent attracts **flies** and **other animals** to visit and carry the flower's pollen around to generate new plants.

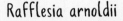

Rafflesia arnoldii

The trap of the pitcher plant

The forest of Borneo is home to many **orchids** that grow on tree trunks. But it is also the home of **carnivorous plants** that **trap** unsuspecting visitors. Such is the case of a species that with its beautiful appearance invites insects and other small animals to visit, which soon turns out to be a trap. Inside its **swollen pitcher** is a **viscous substance** that keeps the unwary, which fall into it, from escaping. In this way, the plant completes its diet with all the **nutrients it needs!**

So much life to protect

I could tell you so much more about this enchanting forest, its **elephants**, **rhinoceroses**, largest **butterflies** in the world, **clouded leopards**, **hornbills** with great beaks, and many others. However, our journey continues **to other places** which, like this one, must be protected for all the species that live there and make these places unique and magical!

ASIA

 Air temperature **2°C**

 Annual rainfall **270 mm**

The phenomenon of ice fog is also called 'diamond dust'

Grand spaces

The **steppe** is an immense plain where you will not see any trees. Here everything is flat where only **herbaceous plants** thrive, attracting over the centuries large herbivores, such as **bison**, which have now disappeared. Other herbivores, such as the **horse**, **encountered humans** in these lands, giving birth to a long history between the two species.

Przewalski's horse is a small wild horse in danger of extinction

Very hot and very cold

In the **steppes of Mongolia**, summer and winter **temperatures** are truly **extreme**. Temperatures range from +30°C in summer to -40°C in winter! But what we may feel on our skin is often different from what the thermometer shows: **winter** is **very dry** and the lack of humidity makes these low temperatures more **bearable**. If the humidity were higher, a sort of **icy mist** would form close to the ground from the encounter of air at different temperatures. In this case we would feel the cold much more!

Life in a tent

One-third of the Mongolian population lives in the **steppes** and is **nomadic**, meaning that they move regularly according to what nature makes available. They are a people of **ranchers**, because their land does not lend itself to being cultivated. Mongolian nomads live in **traditional circular-shaped tents** called *ger*. Although very large, these gers can be dismantled and reassembled in a couple of hours by expert hands! The Mongolian people are **very hospitable**. They also appreciate that their **traditions are respected** even by visitors: one must always cross the threshold of a place with the right foot and accept gifts with the right hand, while the left must support the right arm (and never the reverse order!). But above all, remember that **you should never knock!**

Ancient laws

The more difficult the environmental conditions become, the **greater the bond created between humans and nature**. Here, in a vast territory like the Mongolian steppes, the great **Genghis Khan** in his **code of laws**, written more than 800 years ago, had already created **rules to protect the environment**. Just imagine, for example, **severe penalties** were imposed on those who caused damage to the prairies or started a fire. It was also forbidden to wash clothes in the rivers, to avoid polluting the waters.

Visions from above

Among the species of cranes existing in the world, the **Siberian crane is the most exigent**: it needs a very specific place to live. As a **migratory species**, in fact, it comes to Mongolia in spring to nest, moving elsewhere the rest of the year. It is completely **white** with a sort of **red mask** that extends above the eyes, and has a melodious song that resembles the sound of a **flute**. It has a **serrated beak** that allows it to feed on roots or viscous prey, which is not always easy for other birds. In Mongolia we also find large birds of prey, such as the **steppe eagle** and the **saker falcon**, in danger because of habitat degradation and the toll taken on its use in falconry.

A sea of grass

At first glance, the landscape here can seem somewhat **unvaried**. In reality, however, in the extensive prairies of Mongolia **very different plant species** are hidden, until flowering distinguishes them in colours. There are the white-pink flowers of the **rhubarb**, the yellow of the small **ephedra**, the orange-red of the **lilies** and the pink shades of the **peony**. Many of these flowers are quite famous, because they are also cultivated in the West, or for their healing properties. Looking towards the mountains there are species here that are also found in the Alps, such as **edelweiss** and **aster**. Similar environmental conditions link even geographically distant lands!

Key species

The Alps and Mongolia have another point in common: the **marmot** that lives in the steppes of Mongolia is a 'cousin' of the marmot that lives in the Alps. This large rodent digs burrows underground thanks to its sturdy legs **and strong claws**, permitting other animals to 'borrow' these burrows for shelter once abandoned. The marmot's digging **mixes** the soil, making it more **fertile**. Too often, this animal has been **hunted** for food or to obtain a **curative oil** that is still **marketed** all over the world today. Much of the ecological balance in the Mongolian steppe depends on the presence of the marmot.

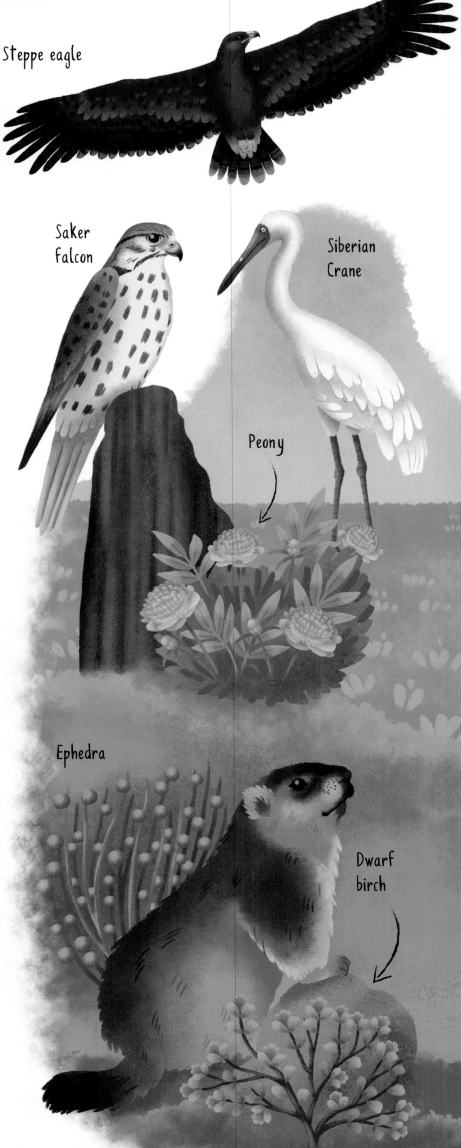

Steppe eagle

Saker Falcon

Siberian Crane

Peony

Ephedra

Dwarf birch

According to some hypotheses, the creature that gave birth to the legend of the yeti is the Tibetan blue bear. Difficult to find, it is a subspecies of the brown bear

Sacred and legendary animals

Certain animals enjoy **particular respect** among the local human population. Some, raised by humans, are closely **linked** to the life and survival of **nomadic peoples**: the **horse**, **camel**, **yak**, **goat** and **sheep**, to which a particular healing power is attributed. Others, however, are **legendary creatures** who arouse wonder and fear. This is the case of the **Blue Wolf**, ancestor of ruler Genghis Khan, and of the **Yeti**, the mysterious 'wild man' of the mountains, fleeing any human contact. Legends and truths highlight the **close relationship between nomads and animals**, between humans and nature: the respect that should be reserved for every creature on the planet.

Yak

Pallas's cat

Elusive felines

Approaching the **hilly slopes**, with great luck you might spot two splendid solitary felines: **Pallas's cat** and the **snow leopard**. The first is small in size, has a flattened muzzle, small ears and thick fur to protect itself from the cold; its **short legs** prevent it from being a skilled runner, and for this reason it prefers to **ambush** its prey. The snow leopard, on the other hand, is a skilled runner, and its long tail allows it to **maintain its balance** during raids; when at rest, it uses its tail to cover itself for warmth in the cold winter, just like a **warm scarf**. These animals have become **rare**, especially the snow leopard, because of environmental imbalances humans have caused, driving these precious creatures to the brink of extinction.

Snow leopard

OCEANIA

🌡️	Air temperature	**12-13°C**
〰️	Water temperature	**10-14°C**

Travelling through time

Here we are in **New Zealand**, a country made up of two main islands. Nature often creates incredible landscapes that leave us breathless. Here we can delve into the depths of the earth in a network of about **400 caves** dug by the force of erosion of the Pacific Ocean almost **30 million years ago**.
My species at the time was almost certainly already present on the planet, while humans arrived much later. I will introduce you to one of these caves, **Waitomo**, fascinating from different points of view.

And now we go underground, but not to worry, we won't be in the dark!

Water that transforms

This cave owes its name to two words belonging to the local language: *wai* means **'water'** and *tomo* **'cavity'**. This place, dug out by ocean water, is also closely linked to water because of a **freshwater stream** that flows through most of its caverns. This slow flow over time continues to **transform the cave** day after day. In the incredible history of our planet, there is **nothing definitive!**

Strange rock figures

The slow and continuous dripping of water inside the caves forms truly **special constructions**. The water brings with it **minerals** that are deposited over time and create **sculptures** that can **descend from above**, covering the vault of the cave, or **rise from below**. These two can also join to form a single **rock column**. It is very important **never to touch** the walls of the caves or these sculptures, because you would transfer an oily waterproof substance present on your hands to the rock, blocking the water from depositing its building material and **preventing the sculptures from continuing to take shape** under the action of the minerals and time.

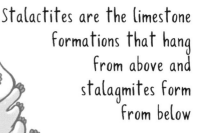

Stalactites are the limestone formations that hang from above and stalagmites form from below

Unknown worlds

These caves remained **unknown until the end of the 1800s**, when a Maori chief and an Englishman decided to explore the intricate underground labyrinths. They embarked on the journey aboard a **raft** and then continued on foot in the lower levels. They were fascinated by what they saw, and still today **many visitors**, even from far away, come specifically to visit this **underground world**.

The stars of the cave

Without a shadow of a doubt, the **centre of attention** of the cave for visitors from all over the world are these special **insects in the larval stage**, which, mistakenly, are called 'glowworms'. What do they do inside the cave? They reside **on the cave ceiling** and **walls**, emitting a **blue-green light** to capture unsuspecting insects attracted to the spectacle. In addition to the light, they produce 'nets' **similar to cobwebs**, to trap any 'passers-by', dazzled by the lights, in a viscous trap. This starry sky **fascinates** not only the **insects' prey** but also the **visiting audiences** to the cave, who are left speechless in amazement!

Adult

In the dark

Living in a cave is **not easy at all**. Without the extraordinary abilities of the 'glowworms', there is no choice but to stay out or to adapt to **living in the dark**. In truth, even the 'glowworms' do not spend their entire life in darkness, but when adult and able to fly, they are **happy to head for the sunlight!** In fact, many animals use these 'inhospitable' caves for only **part of their life**. Others use them as temporary shelters, some for one night, some for a season to 'hibernate' from the cold. There are also animals that **live their lives** in these environments and are often albino, that is, they lack any pigmentation as there is no need to protect themselves from the sun's rays. They adore **high levels of humidity** that the cave is able to give and keep constant over time. I certainly wouldn't disagree with that, you know!

New Zealand long-fin eel

What do they eat?

If you think about a forest, it is easy to identify prey and predators and the entire food chain. Little is known about the cave, but it works the same way: **at the base** of the food chain there are small organisms called **'bacteria'** that draw **nourishment from the rocks**. In turn, some organisms eat bacteria, and animals that live in mud, such as **earthworms**, are eaten by **centipedes**, **spiders** and **insects**, which are the real cave leaders! To keep an environment functioning, **all the links in the chain** are necessary, or life would stop functioning, and a lifeless cave would be even darker.

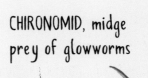

CHIRONOMID, midge prey of glowworms

Cave cricket

The moa was a ground bird that measured up to 3.6 m tall!

Opiliones are similar to spiders and are the predators of glowworms

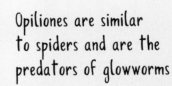

Inhabitants of the past

In the **landscape of a time** not too distant from our own, we would have found an animal wandering in the forests that has become a symbol of New Zealand: the **moa**. This large bird, **similar to an ostrich**, probably became **extinct** about 200–300 years ago because of persecution by humans and the destruction of its home. The moa traditionally **nested** in **caves** such as Waitomo and there are cases of it **having fallen** in without means of escape. That's right, like the ostrich, the moa **couldn't fly!** That is why some fossil remains of bones have been found in caves like this one and in others in the area.

Wonders to be observed with care

As you have probably figured out by now, in a fragile place it doesn't take much to bring an ecosystem crashing down. **Tourism** provides work to the community, but it can pose a **major threat** to the very place itself. We need to find **the right balance** to keep alive a unique ecosystem and sustain the local population.

OCEANIA

Discovering the Great Barrier Reef north of Australia. More than 1,500 species of fish swim here!

 Air temperature **24.7°C**

 Water temperature **26°C**

 Annual rainfall **2,300 mm**

A 'great' space visible from Space

The Australian coral reef is not called 'great' for nothing: it is **more than 2,000 km long** and comprises a vast area of the Pacific Ocean, including islands, coastal areas and a multitude of individual reefs that form a **single complex ecosystem**. But it is not only this that makes it 'great': there are also the **innumerable animal and plant species**, often unique in the world, that populate it and depend on each other. It is an enormous biological structure that is even **visible from Space** and that we have perhaps underestimated! A group of scientists recently discovered a real **underwater tower** made up entirely of coral, which would enrich this massive environment even more.

Submerged lands

At a time **11,000 years ago**, in the area now submerged, small marsupials used to run, known as **wallabies**, which are still present in Australia. A little while after ('little' time in geological terms but 'a lot' of time from our human perspective), the last **glacial age** occurred, which led the seas and oceans to rise and submerge different areas of the planet. It was at that time **Australia split from New Guinea** and the coral reef began to form.

Indo-Pacific sailfish

Australian giant cuttlefish

Team life

Coral are a **colony of tiny creatures** that form a **complex structure** capable of hosting many other species. To develop and thrive, this structure requires **special conditions**. It needs a surface to take root, in places where the water is **clear, not very salty** and very **rich in nutrients**. Further, the water temperature must not undergo severe changes and remain **between 23°C and 28°C**.

Domestic partnership

All this beauty attracts many **visitors** from all over the world every year, bringing economic wealth to local populations. The Australian coral reef, in fact, is **one of the most visited places in the world**, but also one of the most protected. **Biologists and environmental organizations** work here, and everyone does their part to safeguard individual species, knowing that, within the **complex game of balances** of the coral reef, by helping one the others will also benefit.

Giant manta ray, lives up to 70-80 years!

Green sea turtle

Moorish idol

Blue tang surgeonfish

Perfect collaboration

In the coral reef, each organism carries out **its task** around the rigid structures of calcium carbonate created and inhabited by tiny polyps, equipped with **many mouths** ready to suck up the food floating in the water and with **tentacles** to immobilize and capture prey. They might look like bushes anchored to the ocean floor, but they are **animals** that have decided to live all together in large colonies. Among the coral you can also observe other strange creatures, such as **sponges**, which have the ability to **crumble rocks** creating new spaces, hidden where the water is cooler during the day and warmer at night, where many of these creatures of the barrier find shelter.

The noises of home

Don't think for a second that silence reigns underwater. On the contrary, there are **many sounds**! The **clownfish** snaps its jaws to ward off intruders. The male **toadfish**, on the other hand, makes a 'foghorn' sound to attract a mate. Still others **croak** like frogs, **grunt**, drum, shoot... an incredible collection of sounds! When young fish are carried away by the currents, they **find their way home** to the reef thanks to these sounds.

Dream on a summer night

When the ocean and moon align on a magical summer night, **love takes over**. In order for the coral reef to live and expand, it needs to 'bud', to create **new life**, and it does so by setting **biological clocks**. In a night, **clouds of cells** are created that encounter each other and give life to new organisms. If the meeting is fortunate, after five days a **very young polyp** anchors to the ground and creates a new colony. When a colony dies, the coral turns to **sand** and goes on to construct **coral islets**.

Conger eels

Grazing at the coast

As on land, there are **underwater prairies** that grow a short distance from the coast, where the waters are shallow. Here **aquatic plants** provide nourishment to numerous species, such as **sea turtles** and **dugongs**. The dugong is certainly the largest animal that dwells here: it grazes on the seabed ploughing it and making it ready for other vegetation. At the shore, we find an area composed mainly of **mangroves**, home to such creatures as **saltwater crocodiles**, **fruit bats** and **green sea turtles**. Young fish also rest here before returning to the reef.

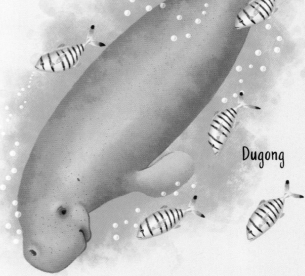

The dugong can be confused with another animal we've already met: the manatee. To identify them, look at the tail!

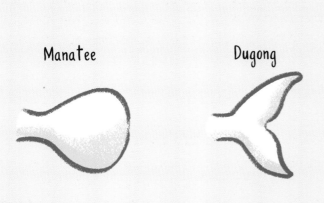

Manatee   Dugong

Dugong

A safe island

In the northern part of the coral reef there is an **island** that serves as a **landing place for green sea turtles**. More than **20,000 turtles** arrive here every year and return with a very specific purpose: to **lay their eggs**. They dig holes in the sand and lay lots of eggs each day. The eggs will hatch **at night**, thus avoiding some dangerous flying predators. Moving in the sand is not at all easy for the new born and reaching the ocean is even less so. It is true that there are many, but **only a few** (just one in a million) will be able to **reach adulthood. After 30 years**, the females of the species return to the island where they were born to lay their eggs in turn. Researchers try to **keep the island unharmed** to allow the return of new generations.

A weak barrier

This large structure is **fragile** and there are many problems that threaten its survival. The **fertilizers** used by the sugar cane industries upset the delicate balance of the ecosystem, where the **crown-of-thorns starfish** proliferates and feeds on the coral, leading to coral death. **Climate change** also plays a fundamental role in the disappearance of the barrier: increasingly **extreme weather events** damage it, often irreparably, and endanger the many creatures that populate it. Further, the **ever-increasing temperatures** cause the algae to abandon the coral colonies. It is algae that live in symbiosis with the polyps of the barrier, providing colour and nutrients through the process of photosynthesis: without algae the coral reef dies.

When a coral reef dies, it turns white. This phenomenon is called coral bleaching

ANTARCTICA

The McMurdo dry valleys are one of the most inhospitable places on the earth. But there are many organisms that have adapted to live here!

 Air temperature   **-15°C**

 Water temperature   **-0.5°C**

 Annual rainfall   **0 mm**

Record-breaking desert

This time I will take you to discover a **truly inhospitable** place located in the far south of the world. **Antarctica** is a region on the planet where most of you humans will never venture. But did you know that within this continent are the **driest valleys on Earth**? It seems incredible because you may imagine the South Pole perpetually covered by ice. Here, however, is the **driest desert in the world**, where it never rains, it never snows, humidity is practically absent and temperatures are the most rigid!

A little air

What is not at rest here is the **wind**. It blows powerfully strong, reaching **300 km/h** and beyond! And it is precisely this wind that is responsible for the **dryness of the area**, because it prevents the formation of clouds capable of generating precipitation. Known as **'fall'** winds, this type of wind forms on the ice hills near the **McMurdo** valleys. There is no snow here and the earth is completely bare. It is a place reminiscent of the **planet Mars**, so much so that astronauts use it as a training ground before missions.

Suspended landscape

These lands, so inhospitable today, once contained **marshes and forests full of life**. But as often happens, **geology** and **changes in climate** play strange tricks. Antarctica separated from Gondwana (the supercontinent that once contained the continents) and began to change on its own. In these valleys, **time seems to have stopped**: there is no precipitation to change the appearance of the place, there is no erosion. The landscape seems **suspended** in time.

Tough life

As you can imagine, life here is **reduced to a minimum**, reserved only for the hardiest, concentrated in **specific areas** and during the **summer season**, when temperatures reach 15°C. In **rock crevices exposed to the sun** and protected from the winds, where a little water is able to form, life can develop. These are mostly **small life forms**, like me, or even smaller ones, invisible to the human eye, but there are also such **plants** as algae, mosses and lichens.

90 million years ago the land was arranged differently and there were tropical forests in Antarctica

Waterfall of blood

In the interior of the valleys there is a **rather strange formation**, discovered for the first time in **1911**. An icy wall on which **blood** seems to flow stands out against the white: a motionless cascade that seems part of a horror film. But there's nothing to be scared of! At first it was thought that the red colour was caused by a certain type of **algae** that lived in the snow. Recent studies, however, have shown that the colour comes **directly from the depths**, where **microorganisms** that live in the absence of light and oxygen have been trapped, drawing energy from minerals such as **sulphur** and **iron**. These bacteria have amazed scientists and are thought to be **ancient** and perfectly adapted to a very difficult life! The colour is due to **iron** which, rising to the surface in contact with the air, oxidizes to become red.

In a black and white landscape... a completely red waterfall!

Nest with an ocean view

Along the coastal area it is possible to spot, during the 'warm season', **animals a bit larger** than those we have talked about so far. Birds such as **Adélie penguins** and snow petrels nest here. Both species come here precisely because these areas **lack snow** which often hinders egg laying. Adélie penguins are among the **smallest** penguins in Antarctica and perhaps this characteristic allows them to move a little less awkwardly on land than their larger relatives.

Adélie penguin

Snow petrel

Password: resilience!

As you may have guessed, to live here you have to be a **superhero** or **superheroine**, to be courageous in order to survive in such dire conditions! The creatures that inhabit the dry valleys must be able to contain the **loss of water**, possess **substances that do not freeze**, viscous like honey, even below zero. They also have to endure, **ceasing certain activities** for extended periods until a minimum of water is available. When conditions improve, during the summer season, there is also the concern of **continuing the species**. Not the easiest place to find a soulmate, it's often **each to its own**.

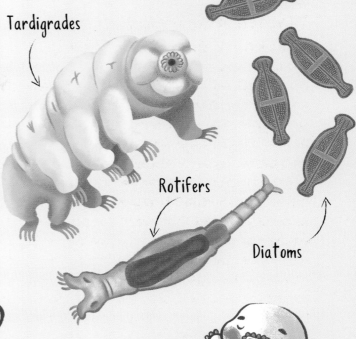

Tardigrades

Rotifers

Diatoms

Since it is difficult to find a mate in this environment, organisms multiply by dividing

Some of the microorganisms that live here

Months of waiting

The only two species of vegetation present in this impossible place are **two small plants** that grow low to the ground. Sticking one's head out too much would be lethal. These plants, and in general all living beings, in addition to enduring **extreme temperatures**, have to cope with the **dark**; for those that draw energy from the sun, it is really difficult to endure months without its light! During the winter, these creatures are able to **adapt to the extreme conditions** of these places and wait for better seasons.

These are the only two plants able to survive

Don Juan Pond is 20 times saltier than sea water!

Underground

Almost as if on purpose, the only **bodies of water** present in the dry valleys are **so salty** they are even **more inhospitable** than the surrounding mainland! **Don Juan Pond** is the **saltiest body of water in the world**, far more than the Dead Sea. The fact that liquid water is available but not useable is a testament to the extreme environment of this region! In fact, **this saltwater does not freeze**, even at temperatures -30°C or -40°C. **There is no life**, apart from tiny creatures on its banks.

Travel notes

Here we are at the **end of our journey** across the six continents of the planet. I have shown you **only some of the many corners of the world**. There are so many more to discover, but I hope I have helped you better understand our **wonderful home** that belongs to all living creatures! As you may have noticed, **geology** and **geography** have influenced the distribution of life on Earth. In every place, even the most inhospitable, **life exists**, and there is a balance among the creatures that populate our world, a **balance** often threatened by humans.

There are creatures, like myself, who manage to **live everywhere** and **adapt** to every change. But we are not that many, and, frankly, I cannot imagine a world populated only by 'superheroes and superheroines'. The **presence of all living species** is necessary to make our planet function at its best. Imagine removing even just one species from the picture...this would cause **damage** to other living beings as well, which in turn could **disappear**.

What can we do then? **Get to know and make known** our home and take care of each of its inhabitants, of each kingdom and every species.

Before saying goodbye, I wanted to share with you some of my **favourite memories** of our wonderful journey together through these different **ecosystems of the earth**.

Tardigrade

Rotifer

The coldest place I have ever visited

The hottest place I have ever visited

McMurdo Dry Valleys

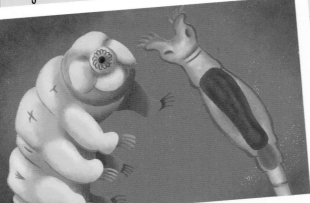

I met this friend in the Dry Valleys of Antarctica, we are both small and resilient

Amazon River

Species that live far apart but share similar climates:
the edelweiss I have seen in the European Alps and in the steppes of Mongolia

60

Fragile creatures

The mission of the **IUCN**, International Union for Conservation of Nature, is to **conserve nature**. The scientists of the IUCN have created a scaled **'red list'** of living creatures **at risk of extinction**. An animal or plant placed in the LC (least concern) category is still at low risk, but as you go up the scale the **critical risk** increases, passing to **categories of greater threat**: VU vulnerable, EN endangered and CR critical. The next step is inescapable **extinction**, first in nature and then from the entire earth.

CR Orangutan

LC Nerpa

VU Giant tortoise

EN Giant otter

Barrier Reef

Iceland

Biodiversity

Biodiversity is **being many, being different** and being able to diversify, each based on one's own qualities and possibilities. And if each manages to stay in **balance**, the **ecosystem works**, the house is home for everyone!

Ecosystem

From this journey I learned that an **ecosystem** is a group of **all the living beings** that make up an **environment**, and that it is not just the **physical characteristics** that create the ideal home for individual species, that all other species are needed if we are to survive and thrive. Ecosystems can be **large**, such as Madagascar, but also **smaller**, like the caves where crocodiles hide or the sharp rocks on which certain lemurs travel. Your garden is also an ecosystem: **go explore and discover!**

The baobab is the tallest living being I have ever met